CHRISTMAS FOR
T·E·N · F·I·N·G·E·R·S

A first piano book of carols and songs with easy accompaniments

MICHAEL HIGGINS

Illustrations by Rosie Brooks

Performance and backing tracks are available on major
streaming platforms or to download from a companion website:
www.oup.com/christmasftf

OXFORD
UNIVERSITY PRESS

OXFORD
UNIVERSITY PRESS

Great Clarendon Street, Oxford OX2 6DP,
United Kingdom

Oxford University Press is a department of the University of Oxford.
It furthers the University's objective of excellence in research, scholarship,
and education by publishing worldwide. Oxford is a registered trade mark of
Oxford University Press in the UK and in certain other countries

First published 2024

Impression: 1

ISBN 978–0–19–357299–7

Music and text origination by Julia Bovee
Printed in Great Britain

Contents

Several carols appear in two keys, with varied accompaniments, to provide an opportunity for young pianists, when ready, to explore playing familiar material with up to one sharp or flat.

We three kings of Orient are

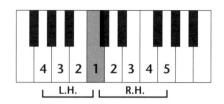

Melody and words by
John Henry Hopkins (1820–91)

With wonder

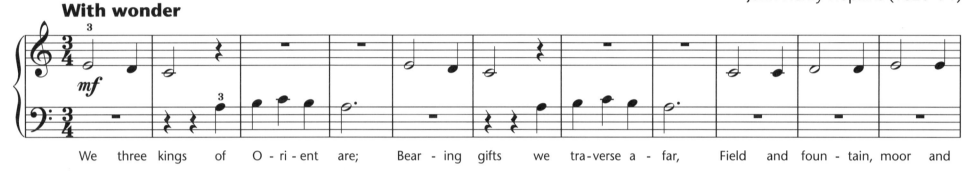

We three kings of O - ri - ent are; Bear - ing gifts we tra - verse a - far, Field and foun - tain, moor and

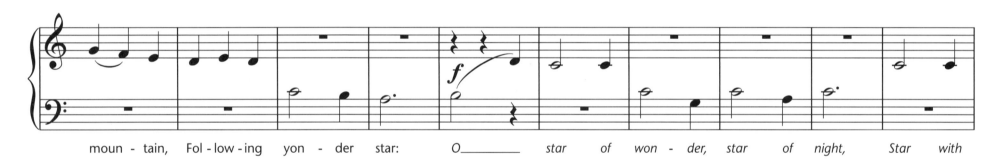

moun - tain, Fol - low - ing yon - der star: O_____ star of won - der, star of night, Star with

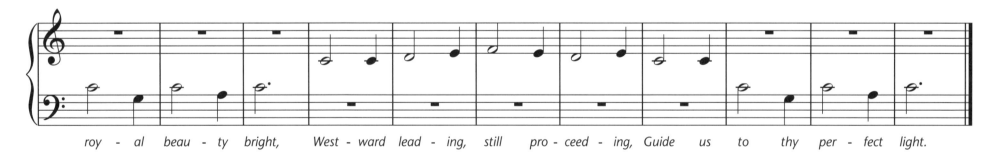

roy - al beau - ty bright, West - ward lead - ing, still pro - ceed - ing, Guide us to thy per - fect light.

Accompaniment

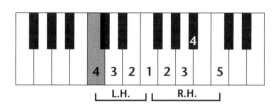

Good King Wenceslas
(F major)

Melody from *Piae Cantiones* (1582)
Words by John Mason Neale (1818–66)

Good King Wen - ces - las looked out   On the Feast of   Ste - phen,   When the snow lay round a-bout,   Deep, and crisp, and   e - ven:

Bright-ly shone the moon that night, Though the frost was   cru - el,   When a poor man came in sight,   Ga-th'ring win - ter   fu - el.

Accompaniment

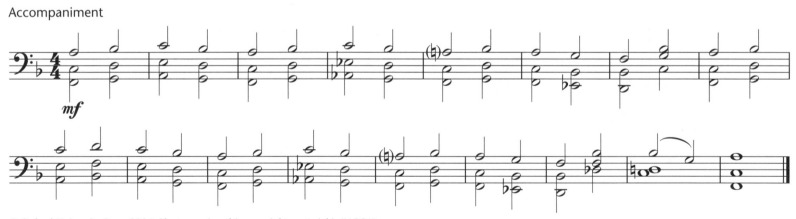

Good King Wenceslas
(C major)

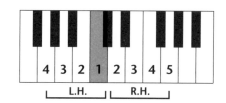

Melody from *Piae Cantiones* (1582)
Words by John Mason Neale (1818–66)

Brightly

Good King Wen - ces - las looked out   On the Feast of   Ste - phen, When the snow lay round a - bout,   Deep, and crisp, and   e - ven:

Bright-ly shone the moon that night, Though the frost was   cru - el,   When a poor man came in sight,   Ga-th'ring win-ter   fu —   el.

Accompaniment

O come, all ye faithful
(G major)

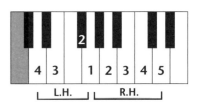

Melody and words by
John Francis Wade (1711–86)
trans. Frederick Oakeley (1802–80)

Joyful and triumphant

O come, all ye faith-ful, Joy-ful and tri-um-phant, O come ye, O come_ ye to Beth - le - hem; Come and be-hold him

Born the King of An - gels; O come, let us a - dore him, O come, let us a - dore him, O come, let us a - dore him,_ Christ_ the Lord!

Accompaniment

O come, all ye faithful
(C major)

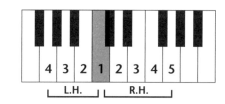

Melody and words by
John Francis Wade (1711–86)
trans. Frederick Oakeley (1802–80)

Joyful and triumphant

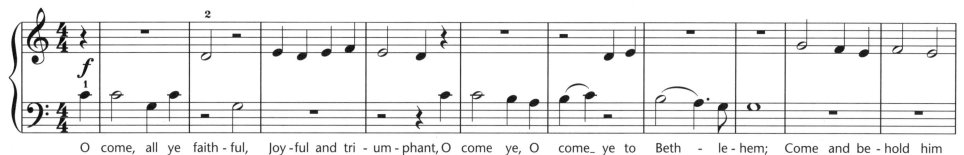

O come, all ye faith-ful, Joy-ful and tri-um-phant, O come ye, O come_ ye to Beth - le-hem; Come and be-hold him

Born the King of An - gels; O come, let us a - dore him, O come, let us a - dore him, O come, let us a - dore him,__ Christ__ the Lord!

Accompaniment

Accompaniment for *Hark! the herald-angels sing*

Hark! the herald-angels sing

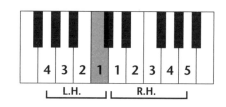

Melody by Felix Mendelssohn (1809–47)
Words by Charles Wesley (1707–88)

Joyful

Hark! the he - rald - an - gels sing__ Glo - ry to the new-born King; Peace on earth and mer - cy mild,__ God and sin - ners

re - con - ciled: Joy - ful all ye na - tions rise,__ Join the tri - umph of the skies,__ With th'an - gel - ic host pro - claim,

Christ is__ born in Beth - le - hem. *Hark! the he - rald - an - gels sing Glo - ry__ to the new - born King.*

Once in royal David's city
(G major)

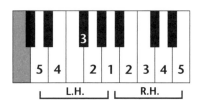

Melody by Henry John Gauntlett (1805–76)
Words by Cecil Frances Alexander (1818–95)

Gently

Once in roy - al Da - vid's_ ci - ty Stood a low - ly cat - tle__ shed, Where a mo - ther laid__ her__ ba - by

In a man - ger for__ his__ bed: Ma - ry was that mo - ther mild, Je - sus Christ her lit - tle__ child.

Accompaniment

Once in royal David's city
(C major)

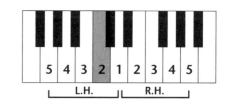

Melody by Henry John Gauntlett (1805–76)
Words by Cecil Frances Alexander (1818–95)

Gently

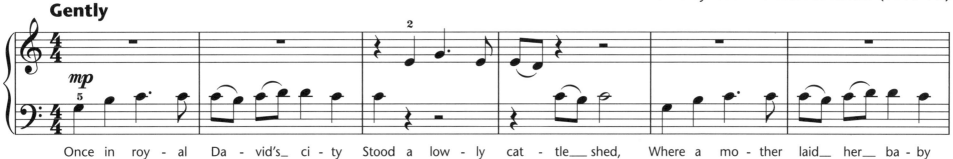

Once in roy - al Da - vid's_ ci - ty Stood a low - ly cat - tle_ shed, Where a mo - ther laid_ her_ ba - by

In a man - ger for_ his_ bed: Ma - ry was that mo - ther mild, Je - sus Christ her lit - tle_ child.

Accompaniment

Jingle, bells

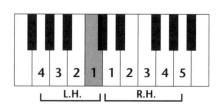

Melody and words by
James Pierpont (1822–93)

Jingling all the way

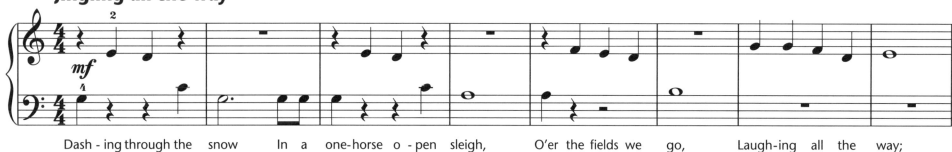

Dash - ing through the snow   In a   one-horse o - pen sleigh,   O'er the fields we   go,   Laugh-ing all   the   way;

Bells on Bob - tail   ring,   Mak - ing spi - rits bright;   What fun it is   to   ride, and sing   a   sleigh-ing song to - night.

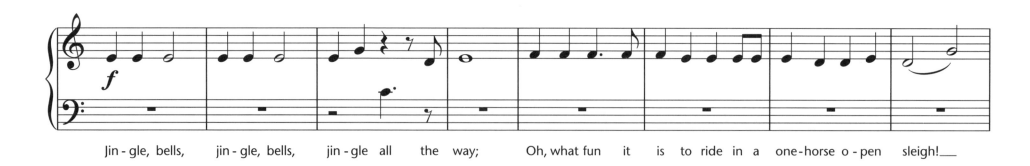

Jin - gle, bells,   jin - gle, bells,   jin - gle all   the   way;   Oh, what fun   it   is to ride in a   one-horse o - pen   sleigh!__

Jin - gle, bells, jin - gle, bells, jin - gle all the way; Oh, what fun it is to ride in a one-horse o - pen sleigh!

Accompaniment: play one or two octaves higher than written

We wish you a merry Christmas
(G major)

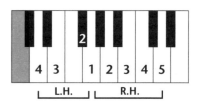

Traditional West country carol

With spirit

We wish you a mer-ry Christ-mas, we wish you a mer-ry Christ-mas, we wish you a mer-ry Christ-mas and a hap-py New Year. Good

rall.

ti - dings we bring to you and your kin; We wish you a mer-ry Christ-mas and a hap-py New Year.

Accompaniment

rall.

We wish you
a merry Christmas
(C major)

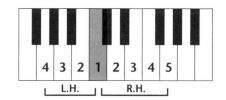

Traditional West country carol

With spirit

We wish you a mer-ry Christ-mas, we wish you a mer-ry Christ-mas, we wish you a mer-ry Christ-mas and a hap-py New Year. Good

rall.

ti-dings we bring to you and your kin; We wish you a mer-ry Christ-mas and a hap-py New Year.

Accompaniment

Away in a manger
(F major)

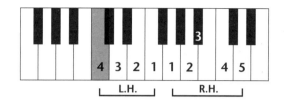

Melody by William J. Kirkpatrick (1838–1921)
Words anon. (19th-cent. American)

A - way in a__ man-ger, no__ crib for a bed, The_ lit-tle Lord Je-sus laid_ down his sweet head; The

stars in the__ bright sky looked_ down where he lay, The_ lit-tle Lord Je-sus a - sleep on the hay.

Accompaniment

Away in a manger
(C major)

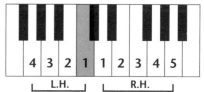

Melody by William J. Kirkpatrick (1838–1921)
Words anon. (19th-cent. American)

Peacefully

Play one octave higher than written when performing with accompaniment

A - way in a___ man-ger, no___ crib for a bed, The___ lit - tle Lord Je - sus laid___ down his sweet head; The

stars in the___ bright sky looked down where he lay, The___ lit - tle Lord Je - sus a - sleep on the hay.

Accompaniment

Joy to the world!

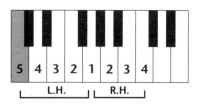

Melody by Lowell Mason (1792–1872) based on G. F. Handel
Words by Isaac Watts (1674–1748)

With joy

Joy to the world! the Lord is come; Let earth re-ceive her King. Let ev-'ry__ heart__ pre-pare_ him_

room,__ And heav'n and na-ture__ sing, and_ heav'n and na-ture_ sing, and_ heav'n_ and heav'n__ and na-ture sing.

Accompaniment

Silent night

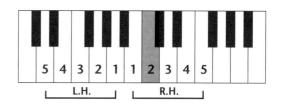

Melody by Franz Gruber (1787–1863)
Words by Josef Mohr (1792–1848)

Gently

Play one octave higher than written when performing with accompaniment

Si - lent night, ho - ly night, All is calm, all is bright; Round yon vir - gin mo - ther and child.

Ho - ly in - fant so ten - der and mild, Sleep in hea - ven - ly peace,____ Sleep__ in hea - ven - ly peace.____

Accompaniment

The first Nowell

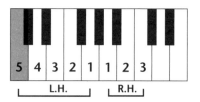

Traditional English carol

The_ first___ No - well the_ an - gel did say   Was to cer - tain poor shep - herds in fields as they lay;   In_
fields_ where_ they   lay,_   keep - ing their sheep,   On a cold win - ter's night_ that was_ so deep: No -

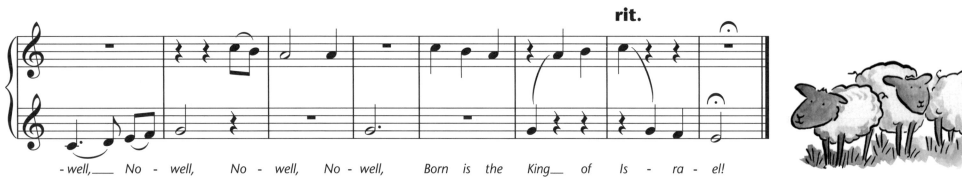

- well,___ No - well,   No - well,   No - well,   Born is the King_ of Is - ra - el!

Accompaniment

O Christmas tree

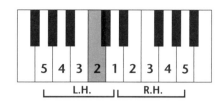

Traditional German carol
Words by Ernst Anschütz, trans. Michael Higgins

Bright and twinkling

O   Christ-mas tree, O Christ-mas tree, how love-ly are your bran-ches. O   Christ-mas tree, O Christ-mas tree, how love-ly are your bran-ches. Your

boughs are green in   sum-mer bright, and through the win-ter   snow-y white. O   Christ-mas tree, O   Christ-mas tree, how love-ly are your bran-ches.

Accompaniment: play one octave higher than written

24

Frosty the snowman

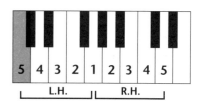

Melody by Steve Nelson
Words by Walter E. 'Jack' Rollins

Jolly

Frost - y the snow - man was a jol - ly hap - py soul, With a corn - cob pipe and a
Frost - y the snow - man knew the sun was hot that day, So he said 'Let's run and we'll

but - ton nose and two eyes made out of coal.
have some fun now be -   - fore I melt a - way.'

Accompaniment